Making Money Doing Entry Online
By Alex Simpson

International Copyright 2012 all rights reserved no reproduction in full or in part allowed. No derivative works based on this information allowed. No resell rights allowed or granted. If you do not agree to these terms close this book now and delete it before reading it. Violations of any of these terms will result in at least $50,000 in liquidated damages plus any and all costs for litigation including travel & attorney fees.

LEGAL DISCLAIMER

DISCLAIMER: The information herein is protected under international copyright law. Any reproduction in whole or in part will be prosecuted to the fullest extent of the law. Additionally, this information is provided with no warranties or guarantees.

A. Simpson accepts NO liability for any losses or consequences as a result of

B. your use of any information herein. If you do not agree with the above, close this book now and delete it! Your download and use of this information constitutes your acceptance to these terms and is considered a binding contract!

INTRODUCTION

Congratulations and thank you for purchasing my book! You are about to gain valuable knowledge on how to make money from home doing data entry! This info package you bought contains a short but very valuable book on making a great income. I am

sure that if you just apply yourself this <u>WILL</u> work for you. Now, before I begin to tell you the actual information & methods to making a living doing data entry, let me say that you are going to have to do some actual work and learn some things. If you're looking to be able to make money by sitting around doing nothing, keep looking! Additionally, you are actually going to have to read this entire book! I mean really, how could you expect to profit from my firsthand knowledge if you don't have the drive to even read this information all the way through?

Now, I have composed a list of legitimate websites that hire agents to do data entry from home. All you need is pretty much a computer with internet access and the will to actually do some work. This is no scam; believe me I've come across a few and I know how frustrating and head popping they can be. I have done extensive research and I can guarantee that these sites that I'm about to show you are legitimate! They don't require you to pay for anything all you do is fill out their applications or send them an email and that's how you sign up. Some of the companies may require that you complete a typing test online. Some of those requirements may be around 30 to 50 words per minute and for some jobs, especially transcription jobs the keystrokes per minute may be even higher. Working from home as a data entry operator is ideal for those who have small children or want to work from their home office or maybe your just looking for a second job, whatever your situation. Make sure that you read the requirements when applying.

So without further delay let me tell you exactly how you will make money at home doing data entry…. Again, let me congratulate you on taking this bull by the horns. It shows that you have the drive & ambition it takes to succeed.

Ok let's begin…

1. http://www.clickworker.com/en/clickworker

Pays up to $9 per hour doing simple tasks, which include data entry for Clickworker from home. Weekly pay. Open to US and non-US residents. A great way to make money from home as many other tasks are also available. The great thing about this company is that you can do this job from anywhere, all that is required is a computer with internet access, no experience is necessary. Sign up and start earning money today!

2. https://workers.virtualbee.com/

They have a test that you will take online in completion of your application process. It may take some time before you hear about the status of your application because they may have a waiting list. They pay by check weekly. All you need is a computer and internet and no experience is necessary.

3. http://www.tdec.com/contact-us/job-opportunities

This company has contractor positions for at home data entry keyers.

Training courses are offered via web conference. You will need a broadband internet access for this position.

4. http://www.gorgewarehouse.com/jobs.htm

This company has several positions available some of which are for data entry operators to post data to their website and database. Flexible schedule. Apply today!

5. http://www.writersresearchgroup.com/company/jobs.html

Although they mainly list jobs in the writing profession, they do have open data entry positions available. You will need to be a quick and accurate typist.

6. https://typists.quicktate.com/transcribers/signup

This company hires typists to transcribe letters, messages, files, etc. You will to have accurate spelling and punctuation.

7. http://www.speakwrite.com/WEB/sw/employment/typist/typist-home.aspx

They hire legal and general typists to work as independent contractors from home. The pay is $10-$12 per hour.

8. http://www.vitac.com/careers/index.asp

Vitac is hiring real-time captioners. You will be required to type at least 50 wpm, have excellent english grammar, pay close attention to details and be able to meet deadlines. Flexible schedules. Apply online today.

9. http://www.dataplus-svc.com/Employment.htm

Data plus has legitimate work from home data entry jobs available. Contractors supply their own computer hardware and software and are responsible for their own insurance, and taxes. Apply online.

10. http://gafundraising.com/

This is a fundraising company that hires data entry keyers to work from home to type in their magazine subscriptions online. There is a waiting list but they do not advertise on their official website for data entry. They pay per piece not per hour weekly direct deposited to your bank account. It is a seasonal job. You can contact them via email and tell them you are interested in the work at home data entry keyer position by typing in gaowebsite@gafundraising.com

11. https://www.mturk.com/mturk/welcome

There are some data entry assignments that you can do from home here.

They pay per task. Fast payout. Sign up today.

12.	http://academicenglishediting.com/files/employment.html

This company is always looking to hire editors to work from home. Please apply or inquire through email.

13. http://www.papercheck.com/editors.html

Looking for qualified editors in all fields of study. They require all applicants to take a 2 part exam and meet the requirements online. You will work in 4 hour shifts and typically earn from $300 - $3,000 per week.

14. http://app.nationalvendor.com/

National Vendor is currently hiring individuals to work from home part time providing data entry and product research for the insurance industry related companies. There is 2 day in house training provided. Must work 30 hours per week from 9 am to 3:30 pm. Pays $10 per hour. Apply online and include your resume.

15. http://landmaninnovations.com/careers/

Landman Innovation is looking for a Denver based data entry professional to work from home to read legal documents, enter data into the spreadsheet, etc. You will need a high school diploma, be a proficient typist, tech savvy, have a computer with Microsoft Excel, have high speed Internet, a have a scanner with a multi-function printer. This is part time and the hours vary. Please submit your resume to careers@landmaninnovations.comResumes should be submitted in PDF format. More details are provided online.

BONUS JOBS FOR YOU!

16. http://www.humanatic.com/pages/userapp.cfm

They have a need for call reviewers to work from home. This is a non phone work from home job. Pay rates increase as you are assigned new categories. Flexible work from home job. Promotions and bonuses are also available. Pays every week direct deposit through your paypal account. I personally work on this website in some of my spare time its pretty good you can earn up to $100 a week if you devout a lot of time to it.

17. http://www.westat.com/index.cfm

There are immediate openings for telephone data collectors for social science research projects. You will ask questions in a variety of subjects such as education, environment, health, and transportation. Must have a clear speaking voice. You will work 15-40 hours per week. You must be 18 years of age. You will need to submit a voice sample, have a web camera, land line phone, strong computer skills, high speed Internet, and more. Go to the careers area to view openings.

18. http://www.apple.com/jobs/us/aha.html

Apple is hiring at home advisors in several states across the United States. Apply online.

19. http://www.sitel.com/media/workathome

Looking for work at home agents to provide customer service for calls routed to your home office. Calls may involve billing inquiries, account product or service orders, installation scheduling, technical product trouble shooting, etc. They offer paid training, medical and dental benefits, 401 K, hourly pay, vacation and holiday pay. Pays direct deposit or via a debit card. Full and part time shifts available. You will need a computer, high speed Internet, analog or digital land line phone with a quiet work space. Previous customer service experience preferred. Apply online.

20. https://jobs.alpineaccess.com/apply/stages-of-application-process/

Currently hiring work at home phone agents to work full time. You will be responsible for answering telephone calls from their client's customers that want to place orders for products or services or to inquire about orders they have already placed. You will be hired as an employee and entitled to benefits, 401 K, PTO, etc. Analog land line phone, USB headset, and computer with Internet service required. Paid training. Apply online.

IN CLOSING

Hopefully by now you're excited and ready to start taking massive action on what you have read. What you have before you is a blueprint for success but it's up to you to put it into action in order to see results. In this day and age it is entirely possible to make money from home but research and determination is required. I have simplified that process by providing these great opportunities all that is required of you from here on out is to read and act!

To your Success,

Alex Simpson

Email:Lexus572@hotmail.com